# Surely There Is An End

# Surely There Is An End

## understanding the power of expiry dates

Anthony Adefarakan

GLOEM, CANADA

# CONTENTS

Preface   1

Case Study 1   3

Case Study 2   7

Case Study 3   11

Case Study 4   13

Case Study 5   15

Case Study 6   17

Case Study 7   19

Case Study 8   21

Case Study 9   23

Case Study 10   25

Case Study 11   27

Case Study 12   29

CONTENTS

▌Become a Financial Partner with Jesus   33

▌About the Author   35

# Preface

Ecclesiastes 3:1 says *"To everything there is a season, and a time to every purpose under the heaven."*

As far as this world is concerned, there are always two seasons. Examples of such seasons include those mentioned in Genesis 8:22 – seedtime and harvest, cold and heat, summer and winter, day and night.

Also in Ecclesiastes 3:2-8, some of these times are highlighted. They include a time to be born and a time to die; a time to plant and a time to pluck up that which is planted...a time to get and a time to lose; a time to keep and a time to cast away...a time to love and a time to hate etc.

These times and seasons always come in pairs; but they do not occur simultaneously. That is, no two seasons or times can occur together at the same time. They always follow each other. For instance, it is not possible for day and night to co-exist; nor is it possible for planting and harvesting to coincide. The duration of occurrence may be long or short depending on the forces controlling them; however, they can only occur in succession.

How then does this apply to man?

The abode of man is 'under the heaven' and as a result, according to the earlier quoted Ecclesiastes 3:1, all men are under the influence of these times and seasons whether they are conscious of it or not. As long as men continue to exist 'under the heaven', they are bound to experience these times and seasons at one point or the other in their lifetime.

The truth however is some of these seasons could be very frustrating and unpalatable; they are mostly better imagined than experienced. At these times, people find themselves asking all manners of questions; like *'Why Me?' Why did God allow this to happen to me?'* among others.

But you can be sure God always has answers to man's questions; and that is what this book is offering you – God's response to your questions.

Remember He is the Beginning and the Ending. May you hear His voice as you prayerfully, diligently and meditatively consider the following case studies in Jesus' Name. Amen.

Surely there is an End!

Anthony Adefarakan

# Case Study 1

## The Woman with the Issue of Blood

Mark 5:25-34 says:

"Now a certain woman had a flow of blood for twelve years, and had suffered many things from many physicians. She had spent all that she had and was no better, but rather grew worse. When she heard about Jesus, she came behind Him in the crowd and touched His garment; for she said, 'If only I may touch His clothes, I shall be made well.'

Immediately the fountain of her blood was dried up, and she felt in her body that she was healed of her affliction. And Jesus immediately knowing in Himself that power had gone out of Him...said to her, 'Daughter, your faith has made you well. Go in peace, and be healed of your affliction.'"

This woman's story is one of the many shocking stories in the Bible. She did not just bleed for one week, else it would have been termed the normal menstruation period expected of every woman. Her own flow ended up becoming an issue.

However, the Bible says she didn't just sit down looking at herself; she tried getting help from many medical personnel – Physicians. They ran many tests and scans on her; they attempted diagnosing her condition using the various fields of medical practice available; they prescribed so many drugs for her to be healed, and as a matter of fact they employed everything else medicine could offer, but all to no avail. In fact, the Bible says she suffered many things from many physicians and even spent all that she had – her salary, savings, proceeds from her investments, her business capital, loans etc. But instead of seeing any improvement, her condition grew worse. What a frustrating experience!

At this point, she retired to fate; saying to herself, 'Maybe this is my own destiny; let me just wait until there's no blood left in my body. Then it will all be over.'

But in the 12th year when she had literally bled for 144months, she heard about someone called Jesus. She heard about the various miracles He was performing – the blind seeing, the lame walking, mad men regaining sanity etc; she then thought in her heart, 'Despite my stinking state, I will press behind the crowd that is always following Him and touch His garment; and I know I shall be made whole.'

She carried out her plan and immediately the 12 years old issue of blood ceased; and she was completely made whole. Praise Jesus!

Now to this woman's seasons; she had a season of bitterness (sorrow mingled with pain, shame and reproach) which lasted for 12 years. But at the end of this season, she was ushered into a different season of laughter (joy mingled with celebration, restoration, and peace) where all her captivity was turned immediately.

It wasn't recorded that she committed a sin which led to her bleeding; if she had sinned Jesus would have told her to 'go in peace and sin no more', but He only said 'go in peace'.

The greatest testimony in the life of this woman however is not that her flow ceased but that she remained alive until the day of her deliverance. People lose blood and die under 1 hour; but she bled for 4, 380days without dying. That should tell you something right away; it means you are not permitted to die before your day of visitation. No matter how life-threatening your condition is, the Word of God that is forever settled in Heaven says "...surely there is an end, and your expectation shall not be cut off" – Proverbs 23:18.

It took 12 years for the manufactured problem in this woman's life to expire; but the most important thing is that it eventually expired.

Why not touch Jesus too, so that your long standing problem can expire? He is there with you; touch Him in faith and His healing power will flow into your situation now.

**Make this confession:**

"Lord Jesus, I believe you healed the woman with the issue of blood in the Bible; please heal me of my sickness (poverty, disease, problems, and debts) too. I touch You by faith today, let Your healing power flow into my situation and bring about the instant expiration of my problems. Thank You Jesus for healing me. Amen."

Case Study 2

## Job's Ordeal

"Job was a man who lived in the land of Uz, he was blameless and upright, and was one who feared God and shunned evil. He had seven sons and three daughters. His possessions were 7,000 sheep, 3,000 camels, 500 yoke of oxen, 500 female donkeys and a very large household, so that he was the greatest of all the people of the East" - Job 1:1-3.

Attesting to his character, even the Lord told Satan, 'Have you considered My servant Job, that there is none like him on the earth, a blameless and upright man, one who fears God and shuns evil?' (Job 1:8).

From these reports it is obvious that though Job was richly blessed, he wasn't committing sin, neither was he proud, else God would have mentioned it in His remark. But a day came when he lost all he had – including his ten beautiful children. As if that was not enough, verses 7-8 of chapter 2 says '...Satan went out from the presence of the Lord, and struck Job with painful boils from the sole of his feet to the crown of his head. And he took for himself a potsherd with which to scrape himself while he sat in the midst of the ashes.'

His condition became so terrible that his wife preferred to be a widow than seeing him that way – Job 2:9. In fact, when his three friends heard of all that had befallen him, they decided to pay him a visit. Job 2:12-13 says "And when they raised their eyes from afar and did not recognize him, they lifted their voices and wept; and each one tore his robe and sprinkled dust on his head toward heaven. So they sat down with him on the ground seven days and seven nights, and no one spoke a word to him, for they saw that his grief was very great."

Imagine that kind of situation; his case was so devastating that his friends mourned him alive for 7 days and 7 nights – without eating, drinking, moving or speaking. In this present age, when someone dies, the maximum respect we give is a minute silence; and even when paying condolence visits, we still talk. But in Job's case his matter was more than a minute silence, it attracted 10,080 minutes silence. It was that terrible.

So many questions must have come to his mind; he must have asked himself – 'What did I do wrong? Where have I missed it? Is God still loving and caring? among other questions of similar nature. But thank God for him, even when he couldn't get answers to these questions, he trusted God all the same. He encouraged himself in the full assurance that 'his Redeemer liveth' – Job 19:25. He also said certain things in the course of his affliction which are worth noting. For instance, in Job 13:15a he said "Though He slay me, yet will I trust in Him". Also in Job 14:14b, he said "All the days of my appointed time will I wait, till my change comes." In Job 27:5b as well, he said "Till I die, I will not put away my integrity from me". He kept saying these things while his season of affliction lasted. The affliction which started in chapter 1 of the Book of Job continued till chapter 42. He really suffered. But because everything that has a beginning must surely have an end, his season of change finally came. The Lord restored Job's losses when he prayed for his friends (as instructed by the Lord); and he had twice as much as he had before his ordeal. Look at Job 42:11-17 – " Then all his brothers, all his sisters, and all those who had been his acquaintances before, came to him and ate food with him in his house; and they consoled him and comforted him for all the adversity that the Lord had brought upon him. Each one gave him a piece of silver and each a ring of gold. Now the Lord blessed the latter days of Job more than his beginning, for he had 14,000 sheep, 6,000 camels, 1,000 yoke of oxen, and 1,000 female donkeys. He also had 7 sons and 3 daughters... After this, Job lived one hundred and forty years (140 years), and saw his children and grandchildren for four generations. So Job died, old and full of days." What a glorious ending!

The life of Job portrays God as a very compassionate and merciful God – James 5:11. He set him up for a glorious ending and ensured he was sustained till that end manifested. He didn't allow him to die before his day of restoration. And because Job's affliction finally expired and never returned, that's why I know that all your afflictions are expiring today in Jesus' Name.

**<u>Make this confession:</u>**

"God of heaven, in the same way you turned around the captivity of Job, visit me today and let my change come. Give me double for all my losses; and give me long life to enjoy my restoration. Thank You for answering me in Jesus' Name."

# Case Study 3

## The Babylonian Captivity

At a particular time in history, the Lord caused Nebuchadnezzar, King of Babylon to invade Jerusalem and Judah; and he carried the inhabitants of these lands – their kings, princes, priests, prophets, men and everyone else into Babylon as captives in fulfillment of a prophecy – Jeremiah 25:11-12.

But according to Jeremiah 29:4-7, the Lord said all the captives should build houses, dwell in them, plant gardens, get married, give birth and even seek and pray for the peace of their land of captivity. Why? It is simply because it was a divine arrangement with an expiry date.

Among those carried away to Babylon as captives were Daniel, Hananiah, Mishael and Azariah (Daniel 1:6); but they maintained their integrity even in their pitiful state as captives (Daniel 1:8-20).

These captives demonstrated the power of God in the midst of the idolatrous Babylonians. For instance, Daniel survived when thrown into the lions' den and the other three enjoyed the presence of the Fourth Man when thrown into the burning fiery furnace (Daniel 6:16-24; Daniel 3:21-26).

However, in spite of the exploits wrought by these men, they still desired freedom. Because no matter the greatness of a slave's rank, he's still a slave; and no matter the level of prominence achieved in a strange land, a stranger still remains a stranger. For instance, these captives had their musical instruments with them but couldn't play them because they were being asked to play songs of Zion in Babylon (Psalm 137:1-4). Verse 4 says 'How shall we sing the Lord's song in a strange land?' It was not a palatable experience.

This desire for freedom led Daniel to commence a search so as to get the expiry date of their captivity as purposed by God – Daniel 9:2. And he discovered it in Jeremiah 29:10 which says "For thus saith the Lord, that after seventy years be accomplished at Babylon, I will visit you and perform my good word toward you, in causing you to return to this place."

The moment he discovered this he started praying on behalf of his people, reminding God of His plans and promises; telling Him to turn His wrath away from His people in returning them to their land.

Their season of change however came like a dream and they were restored. Psalm 126:-1-2 says "When the Lord turned again the captivity of Zion, we were like them that dream. Then was our mouth filled with laughter, and our tongue filled with singing. Then said they among the heathen, the Lord hath done great things for them.

Our God is a God of integrity. Whatever He speaks must come to pass. In Ezra 2:1-11 at the expiration of their captivity, He brought His people back to their own land. For them, it took 70 years for their manufactured captivity to expire; that was a long time, but the most important thing is that it finally expired. And surely as the Lord lives, you are coming out of your captivity too in Jesus' Name.

**Make this confession:**

"Lord Jesus, please turn my captivity today and restore my glory like that of Zion."

# Case Study 4

## Israel's Bondage in Egypt

In Genesis 15:13-16, the Lord said to Abram; "...know certainly that your descendants will be strangers in a land that is not theirs, and will serve them, and they will afflict them four hundred years. And also the nation whom they serve I will judge; afterward they shall come out with great possessions...in the fourth generation they shall return here".

In fulfilment of this, Joseph was sold to Egypt as a slave. He passed through Potiphar's house, landed in prison and finally became the Prime Minister of Egypt. At that time, there was a famine in the land and the only place where food could be procured was Egypt. As a result of this, his brothers came to meet him for food (not knowing who he was); he gave them food, invited his father, revealed himself to them, introduced them to Pharaoh (the king) and through him, the Israelites started dwelling comfortably in Egypt – Genesis 46: 6-27 and Psalm 105:16-24.

In the process of time, Joseph died, all his brothers and all that generation, but the children of Israel were fruitful and increased abundantly, multiplied and grew exceedingly mighty; and the land was filled with them – Exodus 1:6-7.

However, a time came in verses 8-14 of Exodus chapter 1 when a new king 'who knew not Joseph' came into office. He made life unbearable for the children of Israel. He set taskmasters over them to afflict them with their burdens and he made them to serve with rigor. They suddenly became slaves in Egypt, working under unpalatable conditions.

At this time they must have asked certain questions like:
Where is the God of our fathers – Abraham, Isaac and Jacob?
Where is the result of the covenant God made with them?

Who shall deliver us from this bondage?

When shall this ordeal end? Etc.

But while this was going on, God was strategizing His deliverance plan (unknown to them). He brought forth Moses and made sure he received all the training necessary for the task ahead of him. And at the fullness of time, He commissioned him to deliver the Israelites from the hands of the Egyptians – Exodus 3:10; and after many signs and wonders, they were finally released from their land of bondage, not empty handed but with great possessions just as the Lord told Abraham their father several years ago – Exodus 12:31-42.

Thus the bondage of the Israelites in the land of Egypt terminated after 430 years. Their deliverance came in the fourth generation just as the Lord purposed it – Genesis 15:16.

The season of restoration in this case took 430 years to arrive – a pretty long period to be afflicted. But the most important thing is that the affliction expired. It came to a permanent end.

This should serve as an encouragement to you. If God could turn a 430 years old situation around, how old is your problem that He would not be able to solve it?

**Make this confession:**

"Father, I reverence You for all You did in Egypt for the liberation of Your children; please do much more to my captors so that I also can be free to serve You. This I ask in Jesus' Name."

# Case Study 5

## Hannah's Barrenness

1 Samuel 1:1-19 presents the account of Hannah. She was a barren woman whose condition was not as a result of sin; but it was the Lord Himself Who shut up her womb (verse 5).

Despite her condition, she kept going to Shiloh with the rest of her family to worship God. But she had an adversary called Peninnah who was her mate (her husband's other wife). The Bible recorded that this other woman had children – sons and daughters; and as a result she would always 'provoke her sore, for to make her fret, because the Lord had shut up her womb' – verse 6.

This continued yearly, and as a result Hannah would weep and weep, refusing to eat. In fact, on one occasion when they went to Shiloh to worship, Hannah refused to eat but kept weeping in the bitterness of her soul, crying to God to end her reproach, to the extent that the man of God in charge of the temple thought she was drunk (by reason of her mode of praying). Verse 13 says "Now Hannah spake in her heart, only her lips moved, but her voice was not heard, therefore Eli thought she had been drunken."

However, because the Almighty God is the One Who controls times and seasons, He finally remembered her and opened her womb for conception. Verse 19-20 says '...and Elkanah knew Hannah his wife and the Lord remembered her. Wherefore it came to pass, when the time was come about after Hannah had conceived, that she bare a son, and called his name Samuel, saying: Because I asked him of the Lord.' That was how her reproach ended.

In this case study, Hannah went through hell as a barren woman, especially in the hands of her mate, Peninnah; yet she kept going to Shiloh to worship the Lord. And in one of the Shiloh hours, the Lord brought about the expiration of her barrenness, and she became the mother of the greatest prophet in Israel at that time. By the time God fully compensated her for her affliction, she was referred to as the mother of seven – 1 Samuel 2:5. And that's why I know that everything representing barrenness in your life – be it marital, spiritual, physical, academics, mental, financial or otherwise – will expire now in the Name of Jesus. This is your season of fruitfulness in the Mighty Name of Jesus. Just rejoice and give Him praise; He is turning your situation around now. Hallelujah!

### Make this confession:

"Father, You visited Hannah and gave her a new song; please visit me too and put a permanent end to all my reproaches in Jesus' Name. I also will praise You like she did. Thank You for visiting me."

# Case Study 6

## Rachael's Barrenness

Rachael's case was also that of barrenness. She was married to Jacob together with her sister Leah. She practically watched her sister Leah give birth to seven (7) children without her bringing forth any – Genesis 29:31-35; 30:16-21.

She was definitely not happy about her condition. In fact, there was an occasion when she told her husband, Jacob to give her children or she would die; as if it was his fault (Genesis 30:1-2). She even went further to share her matrimonial bed with her maid, all in the name of getting at least a child from her own side. She was literally acting out of her senses by reason of her condition (Genesis 30:3-8). How can your maid's son be called your son? She did not think in that direction; all she wanted was a child being nursed at her side.

This reproach continued for years. We know it takes nine months for a woman to have a full term pregnancy before delivery; meaning a woman can only give birth once in a year. Then, it follows that Rachael's barrenness was well over nine (9) years, because she watched her sister give birth to seven (7) children and her sister's maid to two (2) children. And there is also a possibility that the spacing of those children was not just one year apart. So Rachael literally saw children all around her without any one being hers. It must have been a very painful experience for her.

This reminds me of a story of a certain woman who was well to do but had no child. She had many crying moments despite her wealth. As a matter of fact, there was a time she came out of her house and saw a hen with many chicks playing around her; she lifted her voice to God and said 'God, look at the number of chicks you have given to this hen, and you haven't given me even one'. As she said this, she wept again. That's exactly how Rachael must have felt looking at all those children playing and running around without her being able to point to even one as her own.

However, her season finally came when her reproach expired. The day she had so much awaited finally came. Genesis 30:22-24 says "And God remembered Rachael, and God hearkened to her; and opened her womb. And she conceived, and bare a son; and said, God hath taken away my reproach. And she called his name Joseph..."

The arrival of Joseph terminated her years of shame and reproach. And that's why I'm praying for you now that surely as the Lord lives, your days of shame and reproach are over in the Name of Jesus. The Lord will also remember you this season and cause the tide to turn in your favour. Your much awaited 'Joseph' is arriving now.

**Make this confession:**

"God of Heaven, please give me a breakthrough that is more than ten breakthroughs combined in the Name of Jesus. Let my morning of joy begin now... Thank You for the arrival of my new season".

## The Famine in Samaria

2 Kings 6:24-30 (TLB) says "...King Ben-hadad of Syria mustered his entire army and besieged Samaria. As a result, there was a great famine in the city, and after a long while even a donkey's head sold for fifty dollars and a pint of dove's dung brought three dollars!..."

If you read the entire story, you would discover that the famine became so severe that women started boiling their children for food. I mean in spite of the labour pains that accompanied the delivery of those children, they became food to their mothers due to the intensity of the famine. Verse 25 also says 'a pint of dove's dung (excreta) brought three dollars'. This means dove's dung became man's food during this season. Even then, the people still needed three dollars to be able to purchase a pint of it. It wasn't funny at all. It was almost becoming hopeless. And to make matters worse, the Syrian soldiers had taken over the gates of the city, which made it impossible for anyone to leave the city for any other place. Anyone who attempted to escape from the land would be killed by the Syrian soldiers. It was a real dilemma.

However, a day came (as prophesied by Elisha) when the siege was over. At the expiration of this long season of famine, the Lord caused two gallons of flour to be sold in the markets of Samaria for a dollar. The tide turned for the inhabitants of Samaria and their season of laughter eventually came (for surely there is an end).

I hereby pray for you in the Name that is above every other name, the siege against your life is over. You are moving out of scarcity into more than enough. Your season of abundance has finally arrived in the Name of Jesus.

**Make this confession:**

"By the power in the Name of Jesus Christ, I command every siege against my family, marriage, finance, place of work, health and ministry to be lifted now. Thank God I'm free at last."

# Case Study 8

## Goliath's threat to Israel

Once upon a time in 1 Samuel 17, the children of Israel engaged the Philistines in battle. Among the Philistines' army was a man called Goliath. He's clearly described in 1Samuel 17:4-7:

'And there went out a champion out of the camp of the Philistines, named Goliath, of Gath, whose height was six cubits and a span. And he had an helmet of brass upon his head, and he was armed with a coat of mail; and the weight of the coat was five thousand shekels of brass. And he had greaves of brass upon his legs, and a target of brass between his shoulders. And the staff of his spear was like a weaver's beam; and his spear's head weighed six hundred shekels of iron; and one bearing a shield went before him.'

This giant so much confounded the entire nation of Israel that they became dismayed and greatly afraid, including King Saul (1 Samuel 17:11).

Verse 16 says 'And the Philistine drew near morning and evening, and presented himself forty days'. That is, he threw the entire nation of Israel – God's own people – into confusion and panic for good forty (40) days.

However, at the end of these days his expiry date came. The Lord raised David who not only killed him but also disconnected his head from his neck, thereby putting a permanent end to his reproach against God's people.

The moment this Philistine champion dropped dead, the other soldiers ran and the Israeli army pursued them. That was how God used David to terminate the reproach of His people. During those forty days of threatening and boasting, Goliath never knew he was about to expire.

He was only permitted to flex his muscles for that period, after which he lost his head.

May all your enemies flee before you in Jesus' Name.

**<u>Make this confession:</u>**

"I receive the grace to kill all the Goliaths stationed along the journey of my life. I overcome them all in Jesus' Name. Amen."

## Joseph's Affliction

At the age of seventeen (17), Joseph had two dreams both of which pointed to the fact that he would someday be greater than his brothers and that they would be compelled to bow before him sometime in the future. These dreams brought him so much joy that he couldn't hide them from his brothers and father – Genesis 37:5-10.

But then, things began to go the other way with him. He was thrown into the pit, and was later sold into slavery by his own blood brothers. In Egypt where he was working as a slave, his master's wife lied against him and without trial or fair hearing, he was thrown into the prison where people who offended the king were kept – Genesis 39:20. Now, in that kind of prison there was no hope of coming out except by royal pardon (amnesty).

Right in that prison, Joseph interpreted the Chief Butler's dream which led to him being restored to his former office. And when the Chief Butler was released, Joseph pleaded with him to tell the king about his case, may be he would order his release too. But for two (2) years, the man forgot about him and didn't even say anything about him to the king.

Joseph must have wondered and asked himself; 'What has happened to my dreams?' 'What has being in prison got to do with my brothers bowing before me?' 'Why all these?' among other questions.

However, his time finally came. His season of bondage ended, and he was liberated. His thirteen (13) years of hatred, pain, shame, reproach and ordeal expired in just one day.

The Lord gave Pharaoh, the king two (2) dreams which only Joseph could interpret (Genesis 41:1-25). He was sent for at once and he clearly interpreted the dreams. As a result, Pharaoh set him over the entire land of Egypt as the Prime Minister. It was only in the throne that Pharaoh was greater than him. He became a ruler in a strange land.

It took good thirteen (13) years for the problems and ordeal of Joseph to expire. That was about 156months of uncertainty, because he assumed the position of a Prime Minister at the age of thirty (30).

Joseph passed through all his tests and came out excellently well (Psalm 105:19). He didn't disgrace the only One Who has the power to fulfill his dreams. He waited patiently for God's right timing, and at the end his dreams came to pass; because his brothers actually bowed before him – Genesis 42:6.

I declare concerning you; your dreams will also come to pass in Jesus' Name.

### Make this confession:

"The same power that fulfilled Joseph's dreams will fulfill mine too. This season marks the end of my toil and affliction. So shall it be in Jesus' Name. Amen."

# Case Study 10

## Jonah's Predicament

An instruction was given to Jonah in Jonah 1:1-2; "...Arise, go to Nineveh, that great city, and cry against it; for their wickedness is come up before me."

Upon hearing this, he arose actually but faced a different direction – Tar' shish. However, along his disobedience journey, the Lord sent out a great wind into the sea, and there was a mighty tempest in the sea, so that the ship was like to be broken – Jonah 1:4. At that point there was pandemonium, and after many abortive attempts to stabilize the ship, the merchants resolved to casting lots.

The lot fell on Jonah and he owned up. He confessed to them and told them the only way out was for them to throw him into the sea. They did as he said and there was a great calm.

However, the Lord had already prepared a great fish to swallow him up – Jonah 1:17; and that was when he entered an unforgettable season of his life. He was in the fish's belly (neither chewed nor digested by the fish). He was very much alive; and out of the fish's belly he cried unto God (Jonah 2:1-7).

While in the fish's belly, he had no idea how the whole matter would turn out; he didn't know the duration of his stay there, he was only crying to God for salvation.

But on the third day, the Lord intervened and commanded the fish to vomit him on a dry land from where he went to Nineveh (where God had initially sent him).

In three (3) days, what seemed to Jonah as the end of the world (the end of his life and ministry) expired. Note that while he was praying in the fish's belly, God didn't respond; and so he must have felt hopeless.

But then, the third day came and he was released to fulfill his assignment.

### Make this confession:

"In the same way the fish vomited Jonah into his purpose, I command every habit, behavior and weakness that has swallowed me up to vomit me now, that I may fulfill my destiny. So be it in Jesus' Name."

# Case Study 11

## Nebuchadnezzar's Experience

King Nebuchadnezzar was a ruler over the kingdom of Babylon. He was a very great king with much influence over the people and he was highly revered.

On a particular day, he walked in the palace and began to say to himself '...Is not this great Babylon that I have built for the house of the kingdom by the might of my power, and for the honour of my majesty?' (Daniel 4:30).

He looked at the greatness of his kingdom and attributed it to the power and honour of his majesty. He had hardly finished speaking when a voice from heaven pronounced a sentence against him. He was to be driven away from men to dwell with the beasts of the field (animals). The voice told him he was going to eat grass as oxen and his body was going to be wet with the dew of heaven till his hairs become grown like eagles' feathers and his nails like birds' claws. As soon as the voice finished speaking, the pronouncement manifested. It happened to him exactly as the voice had told him, and he was driven out into the fields (away from his throne) – Daniel 4: 31-33.

In order to paint a very clear picture of what happened to this king, try and watch any documentary on animals like antelopes, deer, bush bucks etc. You will understand his condition better. I mean he fed on grasses, made sounds like an animal, grew feathers like eagles, had birds' claws and practically dwelt with other animals. He was transferred from human kingdom to the animal kingdom.

This continued for six (6) years without any sign of change. But in the seventh (7th) year, when he had spent 84 months in the animal kingdom, he was visited and restored. The Lord ended his ordeal.

In Daniel 4:34-37 he said "And at the end of the days I Nebuchad-nezzar lifted up mine eyes unto heaven, and mine understanding returned unto me, and I blessed the Most High, and I praised and honoured Him that liveth forever, whose dominion is an everlasting dominion, and His kingdom is from generation to generation...At the same time my reason returned unto me...and I was established in my kingdom, and excellent majesty was added unto me..."

God wanted to teach him a lesson and it took seven years for him to learn it. But the most important thing is that he was finally restored at the expiration of his animalistic season – 'for surely there is an end...' (Proverbs 23:18).

The greatest testimony in this king's case is that nobody thought of enthroning another king while he was away. His throne was preserved for seven (7) years, and when he returned, he simply continued reigning; this time with more honour and majesty.

**Make this confession:**

"Oh Lord, teach me voluntary humility, so that You will not have to humble me forcefully. Please help me regain my lost glory in Jesus' Name."

## The End of all Things

Mathew 24:37-39 says "But as the days of Noah were, so shall also the coming of the Son of man be. For as in the days that were before the flood they were eating and drinking, marrying and giving in marriage, until the day that Noah entered into the ark, and knew not until the flood came and took them all away; so shall also the coming of the Son of man be."

It has been said that whatever has a beginning must surely have an end. For instance, this book started with the preface and now it is ending. In the same way, this present world will end someday. Why? It's simply because it had a beginning – Genesis 1:1.

Jesus said He would come back to harvest the world at His Father's stipulated time. He said His coming would be unannounced (like a thief in the night) and only those prepared for His return would go with Him while those left behind would face the Great Tribulation – Revelation 13:15-18.

We are to be ready at all times because this is not our home; our citizenship is in heaven. With this knowledge of expiration, we should start living with the consciousness that one day, this world will expire, and eternity (which does not expire) will begin.

This eternity however could be in Heaven or in the Lake of Fire. To gain entrance into Heaven, the condition is: 'You must be born again'. That is, you must accept Jesus Christ into your life and start living His kind of life here on earth by the power of His Spirit Who will inevitably lead you to where He is on the last day.

On the other hand, to make it to the Lake of Fire, you must reject the offer of salvation through Jesus Christ and start living contrary to

His kind of life on earth by the deceptive encouragement of the devil. And I can assure you, you will end up with the devil himself. But be rest assured of this, you will not be here forever.

Even if rapture does not take place now, what about you dying? What if you die before the second coming of the Lord? Where will you spend your eternity?

There was an inscription on a certain man's tomb which reads "I was once like you, and one day you will be like me." And that's very true. A day is coming when you will stop living because Ecclesiastes 3:2a says there is a time to be born and a time to die.

The question one may want to ask at this juncture is 'when will the world end?'

Well, the Bible did not give any specific time; and even Jesus Christ Himself said He doesn't know the time, that only His Father knows. However, we were given certain clues which can serve as guides towards us knowing the end. For instance, we were told to consider Noah's time; how everything was moving fine and everyone was going about their activities, whereas their sins were multiplying, until suddenly the flood came and wiped out the people who rejected God's offer of salvation through the ark.

Now consider our own time; are our sins reducing or multiplying? Get a clue from your answer. Let us take the advice of Peter in 1 Peter 4:7; it says "But the end of all things is at hand; be ye therefore sober, and watch unto prayer".

That is the way to end well – be sober and watch unto prayer. May the expiration of this world not bring you eternal sorrow but everlasting joy in Jesus' Name. Surely as the Lord lives, we will make it home on the last day. And I have just prayed for those of us already in Christ Jesus. But if you are still living in sin, the first prayer you will have to say is this: "*Lord Jesus, I am a sinner. Please have mercy on me; forgive me of all my sins, and wash me clean by Your precious Blood of atonement. Come into my life today and take charge of all my affairs. I am Yours and Yours alone. And on the last day, let me be with you in Your Eternal Kingdom. Thank You for saving me."*

Congratulations! You are now born again. An end has just come to your sinful life. Go and sin no more.

### Make this confession:

"Lord Jesus, where you are there I want to be. Please help me to reign with You whenever You return. Thank You because I know You will do just that. Amen."

# Become a Financial Partner with Jesus

At *Global Emancipation Ministries - Calgary*, our mandate is *to liberate men through the knowledge of the Truth* and our mission statement is *creating channels through which men can encounter the Truth*

*[Isaiah 61:1-3; John 8:32, 36; I Thessalonians 5:24]*

**Our Ministerial Activities include** Rural and Urban Evangelical Outreaches, Prison Evangelism, Hospital Ministrations, Mobilization for Missions Support, Teaching of the undiluted Word of God, Scripture-Based Seminars, Discipleship, Training of Field Missionaries and Empowerment of underprivileged ones among other Field Ministerial Tasks.

If you sense the Lord is calling you to reach out to the lost by engaging in any of these activities or by assisting those involved with your resources, please feel free to join us. Let us come together as we take the Gospel of our Lord Jesus Christ to the hurting and forgotten ones.

[Mark 16:15-20].

Please join us in these kingdom projects by making your weekly, monthly, quarterly or annual donations to Global Emancipation Ministries – Calgary.

**You can visit the "GIVE" section on our website, www.gloem.org, to learn about other ways to give.**

For acknowledgement, please advise your donations to us by email: info@gloem.org or emancipation4souls@yahoo.com, and kindly include your details i.e. name, address, email and location. Alternatively, you can simply call +1 587 9735910 to do same.

You can also volunteer your gifts and talents in the service of the Lord through our ministerial platforms regardless of your location. To get information on how to go about this, please visit www.gloem.org and contact us via email: info@gloem.org or emancipation4souls@yahoo.com.

God bless you.

# About the Author

By the special grace of God, **Anthony O. Adefarakan** is the privileged President of **Global Emancipation Ministries - Calgary (GLOEM)** with headquarters in Canada, North America and **Emancipating Truth Ministry International (ETMI)** with headquarters in Nigeria, West Africa.

The Lord called him into the field ministry in February 2008 with the mandate to liberate men through the knowledge of the Truth, and by December 2012 he was ordained and commissioned as the Pioneer Pastor – in – Charge of The Redeemed Christian Church of God, Revelation Parish, Shalom Area under Delta Province III, Nigeria where he served until 1st February 2015 when he officially handed over to a new Pastor in order to focus on his field ministry to which the Lord had earlier called him and for which the authority of the church had already prayed and released him to undertake.

On 29th September 2013, he was awarded a Post Graduate Diploma in Tent – Making Mission from the Redeemed Christian School of Missions, Nigeria (RECSOM, Asaba Campus) where he also had the privilege to train Pastors and Missionaries as a lecturer in 2017.

Since the commissioning of his field ministry in 2015 he has had the opportunity to lead his ministry officers to field ministrations in different Prisons, Hospitals, Orphanages, Rural communities, Camp settlements, Markets, Local churches among other places with great successes on all occasions – such as salvation of sinners, healing of the sick, financial empowerment of mission churches, provision of relief materials to the poor, provision of medical services to the underprivileged, baptism in the Holy Ghost, deliverance from demonic oppression, release of inmates just to mention a few - all to the glory of God Who alone is the Doer.

He is the author of other best-selling titles such as *The Law of Kinds, It's Your Size, The Immutability of God's Counsel, Surely there is an End, Life Applicable lessons from the Book of Ruth, One thing is Needful, Life Applicable Revelations from God's Word* among others.

He is happily married to Ifeoluwa A. Adefarakan and their marriage is fruitful to the glory of God.

**Jesus is his Message, Freedom is the Outcome!**
**Isaiah 61:1-3**

CPSIA information can be obtained
at www.ICGtesting.com
Printed in the USA
LVHW011125090720
660099LV00008B/557